This book belongs to

_____

Important Note

*** Each clue eliminates one picture ***

To make this book reusable, use coins or other small tokens to put over pictures as you eliminate them. Do not cross out pictures with a pencil so that you can enjoy this book throughout the season and year after year.

To see an example broken down into easy to follow steps, see the Strategies and Tips and Example pages at the end of the book.

I SPY

with my little eye something that
1. Is food
2. Is not a fruit
3. Has a bone
4. Does not have steam

I SPY

with my little eye something that
1. Is a living thing
2. Is not an animal
3. Is holding something
4. Is not sitting down

I spied a ham.

I spied a girl holding a plate of pie.

I SPY

with my little eye something that
1. Grows from a plant
2. Does not fall off of a tree
3. Is not a fruit
4. Has yellow

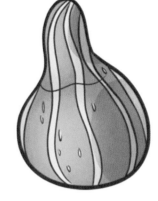

I SPY

with my little eye something that
1. Is not a liquid
2. Is clothing
3. Is not wrapped around a neck
4. Is usually worn only outside

I spied corn.

I spied a jacket.

I SPY

with my little eye something that
1. Is not an animal
2. Can talk
3. Is standing up
4. Is not eating food

I SPY

with my little eye something that
1. Does not have dishes
2. Has arms
3. Is not holding something
4. Is wearing a jacket

I spied a girl holding a plate of corn.

I spied a boy playing in leaves.

I SPY

with my little eye something that
1. Cannot be worn
2. Is not furry
3. Goes with Thanksgiving dinner
4. Is brown

I SPY

with my little eye something that
1. Is not food
2. Has legs
3. Is not wearing a scarf
4. Is holding something

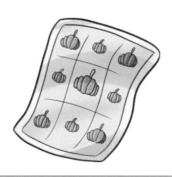

I spied gravy.

I spied a boy holding a rake.

I SPY

with my little eye something that
1. Does not have wings
2. Cannot be worn
3. Grows on a tree
4. Is brown

I SPY

with my little eye something that
1. Is an article of clothing
2. Is usually worn only outside
3. Is not worn on a head
4. Is not worn around a neck

I spied an acorn.

I spied a jacket.

I SPY

with my little eye something that
1. Does not have a heart
2. Can be found on a farm
3. Does not have a face
4. Goes with Thanksgiving dinner

I SPY

with my little eye something that
1. Cannot walk
2. Falls from a tree
3. Is brown
4. Is not a nut

I spied a yam.

I spied a leaf.

I SPY

with my little eye something that
1. Is food
2. Does not have a bone
3. Is a dessert
4. Does not have white

I SPY

with my little eye something that
1. Has a mouth
2. Does not have four legs
3. Is human
4. Is not holding something

I spied an apple pie.

I spied a boy a boy playing in leaves.

I SPY

with my little eye something that
1. Is not manmade
2. Can run
3. Has a tail
4. Not wearing a scarf

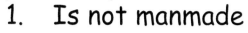

I SPY

with my little eye something that
1. Has orange
2. Is not a rectangle
3. Has two legs
4. Is not an animal

I spied a chipmunk.

I spied a Pilgrim.

I SPY

with my little eye something that
1. Is not a drink
2. Contains brown
3. Is heavy
4. Does not float

I SPY

with my little eye something that
1. Begins with a consonant
2. Does not have long hair
3. Has an open mouth
4. Is not wearing a scarf

I spied a cornucopia.

I spied a boy holding apple cider.

I SPY

with my little eye something that
1. Does not have something you eat
2. Is a living thing
3. Is not human
4. Has leaves

I SPY

with my little eye something that
1. Has eyes
2. Is not sitting
3. Has feathers
4. Does not have green

I spied a tree.

I spied a turkey.

I SPY

with my little eye something that
1. Is an object
2. Does not have a triangular shape
3. Comes from part of a tree
4. Is not small

  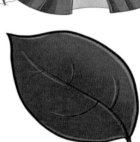

I SPY

with my little eye something that
1. Has blue
2. Does not have yellow
3. Used to keep warm
4. Cannot be worn

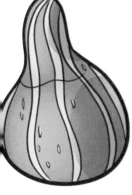 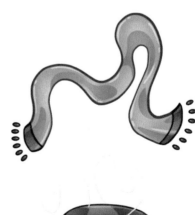

I spied the Mayflower.

I spied hot cocoa.

I SPY

with my little eye something that
1. Can be found outside
2. Has brown
3. Does not have a handle
4. Does not have leaves

I SPY

with my little eye something that
1. Has a pumpkin
2. Is not furry
3. Can talk
4. Is not holding something

I spied a tree without leaves.

I spied a Native American.

I SPY

with my little eye something that
1. Can be eaten
2. Is not meat
3. Is not in a dish
4. Is a dessert

I SPY

with my little eye something that
1. Cannot be opened
2. Contains brown
3. Grows out of the ground
4. Does not have apples

I spied a candy apple.

I spied a tree.

I SPY

with my little eye something that
1. Does not have steam
2. Comes from a tree
3. Does not have a handle
4. Is brown

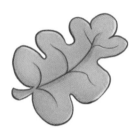

I SPY

with my little eye something that
1. Is not flat
2. Is not a shelter
3. Is produce
4. Is a fruit

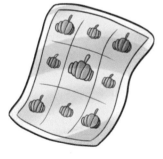

I spied an acorn.

I spied a pumpkin.

I SPY

with my little eye something that
1. Is not hot
2. Has produce
3. Has fruit
4. Is not tall

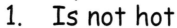

I SPY

with my little eye someone who
1. Is not wearing a scarf
2. Is standing
3. Is holding a rake
4. Is not raking leaves

I spied an apple.

I spied a boy holding a rake.

I SPY

with my little eye a turkey that
1. Is not wearing a hat
2. Has feet hidden
3. Is showing wings
4. Is not holding a sign

I SPY

with my little eye a turkey that
1. Has wings open
2. Is wearing something on its head
3. Is not wearing a headband
4. Is not wearing white

I spied a turkey holding a pumpkin.

I spied a turkey with a Pilgrim hat.

I SPY

with my little eye something that
1. Does not have diamond shapes
2. Has brown
3. Is not liquid
4. Is in a dish

I SPY

with my little eye something that
1. Does not grow on a stalk
2. Is not a plant
3. Has a topping
4. Is a pie

I spied a turkey.

I spied a pumpkin pie.

I SPY

with my little eye someone who
1. Is holding something
2. Is not sitting
3. Is wearing a sweater
4. Does not have a turkey

I SPY

with my little eye someone who
1. Is holding food
2. Has long sleeves
3. Does not have short hair
4. Is not wearing a hat

I spied a girl holding a plate of pumpkin pie.

I spied a girl holding gravy.

STRATEGIES AND TIPS

TIPS:

- Use 8 coins or other small tokens (4 for the first activity on the top half of the page and 4 for the second activity on the bottom half of the page)
- Each activity has 4 clues and each clue eliminates exactly 1 picture
- Read the first clue to determine which picture to eliminate and place a coin over that picture
- Go to the second clue and continue the process for each clue until all clues are read and 4 pictures are covered
- The uncovered picture that remains will be your answer

STRATEGIES:

1. Starting with Clue #1, say the picture name followed by the clue and ask yourself if the answer for that picture is TRUE or FALSE. You should find one that is FALSE.
2. Eliminate the FALSE picture for Clue #1 by covering it with a coin.
3. Move to Clue #2 and repeat the process with each uncovered picture.
4. Do this for each clue until you are left with only one uncovered picture.
5. The uncovered picture will be your answer.

To see this process in action, go to the next page for a step by step example.

Example

I SPY with my little eye something that
1. Does not have a door
2. Does not have red
3. Has four legs
4. Is a living thing

Say the picture name followed by the clue and when you find the statement that is FALSE, cover the picture with a coin.

Clue #1:

The <u>bird</u> does not have a door.	TRUE or FALSE
The <u>rose</u> does not have a door.	TRUE or FALSE
The <u>house</u> does not have a door.	TRUE or FALSE (cover picture
The <u>chair</u> does not have a door.	TRUE or FALSE
The <u>cow</u> does not have a door.	TRUE or FALSE

Clue #2:

The <u>bird</u> does not have red.	TRUE or FALSE
The <u>rose</u> does not have red.	TRUE or FALSE (cover picture
The <u>chair</u> does not have red.	TRUE or FALSE
The <u>cow</u> does not have red.	TRUE or FALSE

Clue #3:

The <u>bird</u> has four legs.	TRUE or FALSE (cover picture
The <u>chair</u> has four legs.	TRUE or FALSE
The <u>cow</u> has four legs.	TRUE or FALSE

Clue #4:

The <u>chair</u> is a living thing.	TRUE or FALSE (cover picture
The <u>cow</u> is a living thing.	TRUE or FALSE

Answer: The last uncovered picture is the <u>cow</u>, and we know that is correct because a cow does not have a door, does not have red has four legs, and is a living thing.

Made in the USA
Monee, IL
13 November 2024

70101046R00026